To Ane,
whom I was lucky enough to help take some of her
first steps.

May this book be a guide for some other first steps
in mountains.

TOUR OF COMBINS

TOUR DES COMBINS

HIKING IN THE ALPS. MULTI DAY TOURS
VOLUME I

Disclaimer

This route involves hiking long distances in high mountain terrain. These areas can be dangerous, specially with bad weather conditions or inadequate equipment or preparation.

Every person who walks in mountains takes responsibility for him/herself and those in his/her group.

The author has made every effort to ensure that the information contained in this book is correct when the book was written. Nevertheless, as this information is subjected to change, the author cannot accept any responsibility for any loss, injure or inconvenience sustained by any person using this book. Also, no responsibility is taken about the exactitude or completeness of the information present in this guide. It is the sole responsibility of the reader to check in advance for information such as transport or accomodation among any other.

The author keeps the right to modify, complete or eliminate any part of this text without previous notice.

References

The author declines all responsibility relative to the contents of the links and references provided in this book.

Rights

The total or partial reproduction, electronic or mechanic of this book is not allowed

©2020 A.C. Cheilon
1st edition February 2020
ISBN 9798613856947

TABLE OF CONTENTS

INTRODUCTION

There are numerous multi day hiking tours in the Alps from hut to hut, well marked and maintained, with easy access and astounding views over mountains, rivers, glaciers, lakes... Unfortunately, most of them are quite unknown while the most popular routes, such as Tour of Mont Blanc and Haute Route are crowded, with literally thousands of hikers every year.

Detailed information about these routes can be much more difficult to find or simply is not available. This book, the first one in the series „Hiking in the Alps. Multi day tours", has been written help the hiker to plan, succesfully complete and enjoy Tour of Combins.

Tour of Combins is a six day closed loop around the massif of the Combins, an extensive glaciated region including several peaks, three of them over 4.000 m: Combin de Grafeneire (4.314 m), Combin de Valsorey (4.183 m) and Combin de la Tsessette (4.143 m). For this reason the name of the tour is Tour of Combins instead of Tour of Combin (Tour des Combins instead of Tour du Combin in French).

Shorter and less demanding than other routes, and not involving hiking on glaciers, it is an excellent option for a first hiking trip in the Alps.

For hikers insterested in a longer route, Tour of Combins can be directly combined with „Tour of Great Dams" (Tour des Grands Barrages) or Haute Route while many other shorter routes can be found a few kilometres away.

The standard hike starts and finishes in Bourg Saint Pierre, a small Swiss village not distant from the Italian border. The first three days take place in Switzerland, crossing the Swiss-Italian border into Italy on the fourth day through Fenêtre de Durand and crossing again on the sixth day into Switzerland through Col du Grand Saint Bernard.
Although sometimes close to glaciers, this route does not include hiking on them, so alpinism gear such as crampons are not needed.

Every stage finishes at a hut or hostel where accomodation and food are available. Most hikers go on a half board (demi-pension) regime that includes dinner, bed and breakfast, so there is no need to carry a tent or other heavy camping material. Some food for picnic at noon can be carried from the beginning of the tour or can be bought at the huts. These mountain chalets are open only between mid june and mid september.

If Bourg Saint Pierre is selected as start and finish point, every stage comprises between 4h 30 min and 7h 30 min hiking time and elevation gains up to almost 1.500 metres. Stages, altitudes and times are described later in this guide both in clockwise and counterclockwise directions.

Other possible acceses are Saint Rhèmy (Italy), Pass du Grand Saint Bernard (on the Swiss-Italian border) or Mauvoisin (Switzerland).

This guide includes not only a description of the route but also information about the surrounding area and many ideas and suggestions to facilitate the planning of the trip. The reader is encouraged to complete the reading of the book before making reservations in the huts or purchasing transport tickets.

Tour of Combins is a very well developed and marked route and huts and roads are not very far away from any point. Nevertheless, this is a demanding high mountain trek involving some days over seven hours hiking. Cold weather and heavy rain can happen and some snow can be found even in july or august. Adequate physical fitness and material are essential.

AUTHOR'S NOTE

Hiking in mountains is a most enjoyable plan for holidays. New places, outstanding views, contact with nature, fresh air, the sense of adventure, sport, starry skies at night... Some years ago, I had some experience hiking, but only for one or two days in a row and when I thought about one week routes in alpine terrain it seemed to me a very difficult enterprise only accesible to extremely fit people and clearly beyond my capabilities. I can now safely say that I was completely wrong. Hut to hut tours such as the one described in this book make several day treks much more accessible, the material to carry is notably lighter, sleeping at night is more comfortable, a shelter is available in case of bad weather... even hot showers and real coffee are sometimes available. Of course a few difficulties remain, but ovecoming them is within reach of almost anybody used to some exercise if minimum cautions are observed.

This book is based on my experience for several years hiking in Switzerland and trekking this route in the summer of 2018 with some friends who came from different cities in Europe.
During the process of planning that trip, I found numerous links, books and blogs about Tour of Mont Blanc, but little information was available about Tour of Combins and other similar routes.

Being familiar with Tour of Mont Blanc, I was very surprised by the fact that other tours are almost unknown while I would say that they are even more impressive. Maybe this absence of information is the reason why Tour of Mont Blanc is quite crowded while only a few hikers can be found on onot mainstream routes.

The idea of helping other hikers to discover these amazing places and share with them some useful tips obtained from my experience is what motivated the writing of this book. I just have tried to write the guide I would have liked to find when I was planning the trip.

One last advice before start: try to learn about mountains. Not considering hiking just a sport will make your trip much more enjoyable. I mean getting some background about geology, mountain formation, glaciers, faune, vegetation... but there is no need to study a bunch of books from the library. Many informative pannels can be found and spending a short time reading them and observing the environment can be a very rewarding activity. With very little effort the hiker will recognise an edelweiss or a myrtille or will be able to say where there was a glacier during the ice ages. Avoid hurrying up, consider time indications as a reference, not a goal. Make some pauses to enjoy the views, take photos, pay attention to the shape of stones, flowers or valleys, look at the glaciers, imagine how they were years ago... if not already, you will probably fall in love with mountains.

PART I

GENERAL INFORMATION

HOW TO GET THERE

There are several options to get to the route and to come back after finishing it. When planning the transportation, it is advisable to spend some time exploring several options and prepare a datasheet to compare. Once decided, it is recommended to keep a list of the transports and timetables (even the following or the previous in case the rythm is different than expected).

The standard hiking route begins and ends in Bourg Saint Pierre (Switzerland).
Col du Grand Saint Bernard or Saint Rhèmy (Italy) are on the same road and can be alternative start and finish points. Mauvoisin is accesible by road too.

BY PLANE

The nearest airports are located in Geneva, Bern and Turin. Milan is also an alternative to explore, because many companies fly to the several airports there. Lyon, Zurich and Basel are farther away but could be considered too.

Access to Bourg Saint Pierre by public transport is very easy from Switzerland and possible but more difficult and time consuming from Italy. From France, the best option is to go via Geneva.

Note: Tables below include highways and country borders. Times are orientative and do not consider traffic jams, maintenance works or others. It is advisable to anticipate some extra time for possible delays, specially for the return trip.

FROM	KM TO BOURG ST PIERRE	TIME BY CAR
Geneva airport (via Switzerland)	163	1h 50 min
Geneva airport (via Chamonix)	170	2h 30 min
Turin airport	160	2h 00 min
Milan Malpensa airport	220	2h 30 min
Milan Linate airport	240	2h 45 min
Milan Bergamo airport	267	3h 00 min
Lyon Airport	310	3h 20 min
Bern airport	170	2h 05 min
Basel airport	265	3h 00 min
Zürich airport	288	3h 00 min

FROM	KM TO ST RHÉMY	TIME BY CAR
Geneva airport	170	2h 30 min
Turin airport	137	1h 35 min
Milan Malpensa airport	200	2h
Milan Linate airport	220	2h 20 min
Milan Bergamo airport	246	2h 35 min
Lyon Airport	295	3h 20 min
Bern airport	192	2h 20 min
Basel airport	288	3h 15min
Zürich airport	311	3h 25 min

FROM	KM TO COL G. SAINT BERNARD	TIME BY CAR
Geneva airport	175	2h
Turin airport	137	1h 35 min
Milan Malpensa airport	207	2h 15 min
Milan Linate airport	227	2h 35 min
Milan Bergamo airport	253	2h 50 min
Lyon Airport	322	3h 30 min
Bern airport	182	2h 15 min
Basel airport	277	3h 10 min
Zürich airport	300	3h 10 min

FROM	KM TO MAUVOISIN	TIME BY CAR
Geneva airport	170	2h 00 min
Turin airport	200	2h 50 min
Milan Malpensa airport	260	3h 30 min
Milan Linate airport	280	3h 40 min
Milan Bergamo airport	310	3h 50 min
Lyon Airport	320	3h 30 min
Bern airport	175	2h 15 min
Basel airport	270	3h 00 min
Zürich airport	290	3h 15 min

If arriving or leaving by plane, most probably it will be necessary to spend at least one night along the way. See the section „Not only the tour" to get some ideas to plan those days, as there are a lot of interesting places in the neighboring area.

For small groups of hikers, renting a car at the airport may be less expensive and more convenient than using public transports.

BY CAR

Bourg Saint Pierre is located on the road from Martigny (Switzerland) to Aosta (Italy). Col du Grand Saint Bernard is on the same road, on the border between both countries and Saint Rhèmy is the first village on the Italian side.

St Rhèmy, Col du Grand Saint Bernard and Mauvoisin are alternative start/finish points.

Mauvoisin is another possible start/finish point, located on a different road and is only accessible from Switzerland.

At Bourg Saint Pierre, St. Rhèmy, Col du Grand St. Bernard and Mauvoisin, parking spots are available. Distances and estimated times from the nearest airports are presented in the previous section.

When travellling from Italy, if the Grand Saint Bernard Pass is open, it is recommended to avoid the tunnel, as it is quite expensive and the drive over the pass is an attraction on its own.

Green signals indicate highways in Switzerland, not blue as in other European countries. A sticker (vignette) must be purchased and attached to the front window of the car in order to use these roads. Cars rented in Switzerland alredy have a vignette but are usually more expensive.

When driving to Martigny from Chamonix (France), and from Martigny to Bourg Saint Pierre or Mauvoisin, no Swiss highways are used.

Note: Insurances for cars rented in Italy or France may not cover Switzerland and vice versa.

BY TRAIN/BUS

Travelling by public transport is the most ecological way to access the route. Please, keep it in mind when planning.

During the summer a bus service from Aosta (Italy) to Martigny (Switzerland) and return with stops at Saint Rhèmy, Grand Saint Bernard and Bourg Saint Pierre is available with several daily courses. The last one is late enough for the hikers to complete the final stage on time for the last bus and the first one is early enough to finish the first stage on time for dinner. There is no need to spend a night at Bourg Saint Pierre, Mauvoisin, St Rhémy or Col du Grand Saint Bernard neither at the beginning nor at the end of the tour. Other places like Martigny or Aosta are easy to access and are much more interesting to explore the day before the route or the evening after.

Timetables, trip duration and prices can be found on SBB/CFF website (www.sbb.ch). This website is extremely useful when planning trips in Switzerland and it is strongly advisable to doublecheck the planning and keep a detailed printed timetable.

When planning the first day, it is important to arrive to the hut before 18:30. Hikers arriving late may be denied dinner even with a reservation made. Also, hitchhike or calling a taxi is the only option to return after the last bus has left.

The bus stop at Bourg Saint Pierre is called Bivouac Napoleon (Hotel). Buses usually have screens indicating the names of the stops or the driver can be asked. They generally speak good English and are very helpful.

Note: Big groups may be required to book in buses in advance.

From any place in Switzerland first get to Martigny by train. From there get another train to Le Châble and change at Sembrancher station to get another train to Orsières and there get a bus to Bourg Saint Pierre. Although it may sound like a lot of changes, these lines are coordinated, so from Martigny to Bourg Saint Pierre, even involving two connections, it usually takes less than one hour and a half.

FROM	TO	TRANSPORT	TIME
Anywhere in Switzerland	Martigny	Train	-
Martigny	Sembrancher	Local train 1	16 min
Sembrancher	Orsières	Local train 2	10 min
Orsières	Bourg St Pierre	Bus	25 min

From Lyon, in France, there is a direct train to Geneva and from Geneva there is another direct train to Martigny

FROM	TO	TRANSPORT	TIME
Lyon	Geneva	Train	2h
Geneva	Martigny	Train	1h 40min

From Italy, the city of Aosta (Italy) can be reached by train from Milan or Turin. And then a bus can be taken to the route. A helpful website to find information about transport is www.rome2rio.com

FROM	TO	TRANSPORT	TIME
Milan	Chivasso	Train	1h 20 min
Chivasso	Aosta	Train	1h 20 min
Aosta	Bourg St Pierre	Bus	1h

FROM	TO	TRANSPORT	TIME
Milan	Aosta	Train	2h 30 min
Aosta	Bourg St Pierre	Bus	1h

FROM	TO	TRANSPORT	TIME
Turin	Ivrea	Train	50 min
Ivrea	Aosta	Train	1h 10 min
Aosta	Bourg St Pierre	Bus	1h

FROM	TO	TRANSPORT	TIME
Turin	Aosta	Train	1h 30min
Aosta	Bourg St Pierre	Bus	1h

Note: the direct course Milan-Aosta is not frequent.

Note: for the first option, another change at Ivrea bertween Chivasso and Aosta may be required.

Note: Timetables and courses may differ or not be available on Saturdays and Sundays.

Mauvoisin can only be reached by road from Switzerland. There is a train service from Martigny to Le Châble and then a bus to Mauvoisin (usually for a total of about one hour and a half including the change).

FROM	TO	TRANSPORT	TIME
Martigny	Le Châble	Train	30 min
Le Châble	Mauvoisin	Bus	50 min

Tickets can be bought in advance online at SBB website. Also in Swiss train stations there is sometimes a shop and there are always machines where tickets can be directly bought just selecting origin and destination. A ticket valid from Geneva airport to Bourg Saint Pierre can be obtained even if it includes several trains or buses. Both cash (Swiss francs) and credit cards are accepted by these machines.

On the way back, a ticket for the bus must be directly bought to the bus driver and then the ticket for the train can be bought at the train station. Generally credit cards are not accepted on buses.

On Swiss trains, stopping at intermediate stations is allowed. For example it is possible to buy a ticket from Geneva airport to Martigny and stop in Montreux and then in Lausanne for a few hours. Nevertheless, the ticket is only valid for one day.

Tickets for the train must be obtained in advance, not during the trip. A fine can be imposed to anyone travelling without a valid ticket.

Transport in Switzerland is comfortable and fast but can be really expensive. Some one day travelcards, half price (demi tariff in French) cards and others can be purchased. They are specially interesting for longer distances, for instance when travelling from Basel or Zürich or if the trip includes some extra tourism in Switzerland.
It is advisable to explore in detail the SBB/CFF website.

Note: Trip times in this section do not include changes and waiting time. This information is specially subjected to change, so it should only be used as a reference when planning.

WHEN TO GO

Hiking season in the Alps takes place from mid june to mid september. In june, july and even the beginning of august, some snow may be found covering sections of the path. The exact first and last day of the season depends on the weather, so in june or september, it is recommendable to check the huts websites to make sure that they are open and available before purchasing plane tickets or arranging any other reservation. Occasionally some huts close for the season because of maintenance works. Webpages, telephone numbers and emails are indicated later in this guide.

Although this tour is not crowded as other courses such as Tour of Mont Blanc, in late july and august and on weekends, some huts may be full. Cabane Chanrion is specially popular.

Reservations for the huts must always be made in advance, if possible with at least two weeks. Hikers arriving without booking may be rejected.
Always print and carry a copy of every confirmation, and do not hesitate to e-mail or phone if any of them has not been received.

Temperatures in june and september can be significantly lower than in july. If hiking during these months, some warmer clothes may be needed.

A NORMAL DAY

Usually hikers get up around 7:00 AM, get dressed and are having breakfast around 7:15 or 7:30 AM. Afterwards packing, washing teeth, applying sun protection and getting prepared in order to start the route, if possible before 8:30.

Most groups make short pauses each one or two hours to enjoy the panorama from a viewpoint, take photos, drink, eat or refill the water bottle. About noon, it is time for a longer pause and lunch. Of course, it can be done earlier or later in order to stop at a pass, a hut or some specific point in the route. Some groups prefer shorter pauses while others prefer to rest for a longer time. Anyway, pauses lasting more than one hour and a half should be avoided as it is difficult to restart afterwards.

In the afternoon, the groups continue hiking much like in the morning until they arrive to the end of the stage. Time of arrival depends on the rythm and the stage but it can be said that ordinarily, it happens between 15:00 and 17:00.
Then stretching, taking out the boots and checking in. The hut staff usually assigns a dormitory and even an specific place to the hikers. Generally, backpacks are left near the matresses, the sleeping bags are extended and then the group goes to the living room or the terrace.

Some travellers may be tired and prefer to lay down and perhaps have a nap. There is some time to rest, have a shower (if available), handwash some clothes... until 18:30 or 19:00 when dinner is served.

After dinner, hikers generally stay in the living room playing cards, reading or talking. There some cards, board games and books are available to be borrowed.
At a given time, between 21:30 and 23:00 everybody is expected to be in bed anf lights off.

TRAINING, REQUIRED SKILLS

This tour involves hiking long distances in high mountain terrain. A good physical condition is required to enjoy the tour. Nevertheless, no climbing or glacier experience is needed.

Some hiking on weekends before the tour is recommended. Use the same boots, clothes and try to carry the same baggage even if it is a one day excursion. That will help identify some possible problems that could arise during the trip: clothes that produce blisters, boots that hurt or do not suit...

The path is in general very well marked. Nonetheless, some orientation skills are needed, specially in bad weather conditions. It is advisable to prepare and check GPS systems, maps, compass and other orientation material before arrival.

The hiking rythm is critical. Hiking in mountains, specially during ascents, is completely different from walking in the city because of steep and difficult terrain and heavy backpacks. A slower rythm and shorter steps make a hike much more comfortable. If the rythm forces the hikers to stop to recover breath, it is clearly too fast.

Times indicated in this guide and in the signals are orientative, not a goal. Moreover, trying to hike too fast increases the risk of lesions and can produce much more fatigue and paradoxically slower stages.

EQUIPMENT

It must be light, robust and comfortable. During this tour, over seven hours of hiking on steep, sometimes irregular slopes is required some days. A heavy backpack can make the trip harsh even for fit hikers. Avoid carrying unnecesary items and try to keep the backpack below ten kilograms or even seven if possible.

The most usual problem for hikers are blisters, wounds or other problems in their feet. Inadequate boots and socks are a frequent source of issues.

Recommended gear:
- Backpack: around 35 litres capacity should be enough. It must have a waterproof cover and an adjustable waist-belt.
- Boots. Be sure to use them several times before the tour and check that they can be worn for several hours without producing wounds or pain. Snickers and running shoes are not recommendable given that mud, water and snow could be found.
- T-shirts. They can be hand cleaned and dried if needed at the huts. Three should be enough, two for the days and one for the night. At least one should have long sleeves. Merino wool is preferable to acrylic as it reduces odours.

- Socks. At least three pairs. After a long, cold, rainy day, not having dry socks can be really annoying. Good quality, breathable thick socks are the key to avoid blisters and other feet problems. Always be careful when putting them on. Wrinkles in socks can produce blisters.
- Trousers. A pair to wear and a pair in reserve in case of rain.
- Underwear. Be sure it is comfortable and does not irritate the skin even after several hours of hiking. Three or four pairs should be enough.
- Warm sweater or polar.
- Waterproof warm jacket. The jacket should allow for several hours of rain without getting wet. Rain ponchos will protect both the body and the backpack for hours, although in general they are not breathable or warm at all and require a lot of space.
- Sunglasses (category III or IV)
- Cap or hat for the sun.
- Gloves and hat for cold weather.
- Sleeping bag liner or sheet sleeping bag (sac à viande in French). Mandatory at huts.
- Head light. Useful in dormitories at night.
- Taps for ears. Dormitories at night may be noisy.
- Lipsalve and sun protection (at least factor 30 or higher if hikers tend to get burnt easily). People with very pale skin, should apply it not only once but several times each day. Do not forget ears and nape.

– Walking poles. Very helpful on snow and slippery terrain, they also reduce charge on knees and legs. On planes, they probably will not be accepted as hand luggage.
– Water bottle. At least one litre capacity. Many hikers prefer hydration systems integrated in their backpacks so they do not need to stop to drink. At some huts, hot tea is provided in the morning; make sure that bottles/hydration system can stand hot liquids.
– Picnic. Half board (demi pension) at the huts include dinner and breakfast. Generally they are tasty, abundant and full of energy. Of course, some extra food and drinks can be bought at the huts during the evenings. Also some food for picnic can be purchased, or can be carried from the beginning of the tour to be eaten at noon each day. Food for picnic should be light and full of energy: nuts, energy bars and dry fruit are the most usual options. Dinner at huts usually does not include a lot of fresh fruit of vegetables. Carrying some apples can compensate, but they are heavy. Other fruits such as bananas or tangerines can be an alternative, but they are easily crashed inside the backpack if they are not stored carefully.
– Map, compass and altimeter.
– Tape, needles and some thread can be useful if some minor repair is needed.
– Some small book or cards or similar entertainment for the evenings.

- Toilet paper.
- Mobile telephone. A separate GPS, a GPS app and an extra battery can be useful too. Some charge must always be saved in case an emergency call is needed. See section about Orientation, maps and GPS.
- First aid kit. The most probable issues are blisters or wounds on feet, toes or toe nails: Scissors, sterile gauzes, oxygenated water, medical adhesive tape, adhesive wound-closure strips and blister pads are the minimum. Only one per group. Toe nails should be cut two or three days before starting the tour. Long toe nails can easily break after hours hiking, get purple or hurt.
- Toilet material (toothpaste, deodorant, soap or shower gel...). If distributed among the group members some weight can be reduced. Small plastic bottles like the ones provided in hotels are preferable rather than big ones. A resistant plastic bag is useful to keep all this material separated from the rest of the luggage in case any bottle opens.
- Some plastic bags are useful to keep the food and the dirty clothes separated from the rest of the equipment or for extra protection against rain.
- Passport, cash money, documents, printed booking confirmations, list of useful adresses, telephone numbers and transport, Club Alpin or equivalent card and this book (all of this should be kept in a separate waterproof bag).

Not needed:
- Sleeping bag and tent if the group is sleeping at the mountains huts. This is a huge saving of space and weight. Nevertheless a sleeping bag liner will be needed instead of a regular sleeping bag.
- Camping gas and pot. Of course they can be carried in order to eat some warm food at noon but they are not indispensable.
- Ice axe, rope and crampons. This route does not include hiking on glaciers. Unless some extra excursion is planned, they are not required.
- Sleeping pad. In the dormitories in the huts there are mattresses.
- Portable water treatment systems. Drinkable water is often available along this route from streams or can be bought at Cabane Chanrion, the only hut with no access to drinkable water.

Note: This tour takes place in high mountain terrain, many days at almost 3.000 m. Severe storms, strong winds and cold temperatures may happen and snow may be found on some spots. In addition, weather conditions can change very fast. Sometimes, even experienced hikers forget and underestimate when packing in summer in the city.

Note: always check and use several times, all the material in advance. Specially boots and clothes can be uncomfortable and even produce blisters or chafings when new.

Note: at huts there is a place to hand wash the clothes, usually a large sink in the bathroom, and dry them. It is completely normal and often indicated. If not, do not feel embarrased to ask if you need to wash your clothes. It is advisable to clean them as often as possible, so a reserve is always available.

Note: It is recommendable to prepare a check list and use it when packing.

Note: some hikers experience irritations on groins and armpits due to the continuos movement. Applying some vaseline before the stage, like long distance runners may prevent or reduce these inconveniences.

MOUNTAIN HUTS

In the Alps there are plenty of huts that were initially built for alpinism, as most of the peaks are not reachable in one day. Nowadays they are also used for ski touring in winter and by hikers to avoid carrying a tent or going down to the valley every night.

They are not simple bivouacs, but a sort of small hotels in the mountains, generally built in places with astounding views over glaciers, waterfalls or peaks. Nevertheless they are not standard hotels and some special rules apply. Located in remote areas, where all materials and goods are carried by helicopter, some of them ca be hard to access (ladders or difficult paths can be found).

Most of these huts were built and are maintained by Club Alpin Suisse, Club Alpino Italiano or the equivalent in other countries but some others are privately owned. Being a member of Club Alpin or an associate entity entitles to a discount. It is worth checking with your local organisation as some other advantages as an insurance may be included.

Often mobile coverage is not available, although satellite telephones and/or radios can be used for emergencies. Only cash is accepted at most of the huts and electricity for device charging is not always accessible.

Generally these buildings consist of a small room to leave the boots, a big dinner room with several long tables, toilets, kitchen and a reserved area for the staff and the dormitory or dormitories on the upper floor. Many have a terrace with amazing views.

Reservations must always be done in advance and sometimes the huts are complete. It is better to plan with time and inform of any change of schedule or cancellation. Bookings can be made online by means of a form or via e-mail. Websites are indicated later in this book.

Almost every group of hikers choose a half board regime. It includes dinner, night and breakfast and is strongly recommended as the best option so only food for noon needs to be carried. Dinner is generally served at a fixed time, generally about 18:30 and includes soup, a main course and dessert. Different groups sit down at the same table and the food is shared. There is a closed menu although vegetarian and celiac options sometimes are available on request. Beer, pie, coffee, tea, water and food for picnic can also be purchased.

Usually at the huts, when doing the check in, the hikers will be required to open an account to write down the drinks and food and asked to pay late at night or the following morning before leaving.
Breakfast usually includes bread, jam and butter, cheese and cold sausages, muesli or cereals, milk, tea and coffee and some hot tea is provided to take away (generally one litre per person).

Private rooms for 4 or 6 persons are available at some huts, but generally dormitories (dortoirs in French) are the only option. Up to 20-25 people share a bedroom and sleep side by side with no gender separation. Blankets and matresses are provided and the use of a sac à viande, a kind of light sleeping bag is mandatory. Everybody goes to bed early, and generally no noise is allowed after 21:00 or 22:00 as groups of alpinists often get up as early as 3.00 AM. A head light may be useful during the night if somebody needs to go to the toilet or look for something, because the main light of the bedroom is switched off at night. In the dormitories, try to avoid unnecessary noise or talking and have everything at hand, given that other people will be sleeping.

Toilets at huts are generally basic or very basic. Showers are not always available and if available they are usually cold and at an extra cost. There is almost always a place where some basic clothes cleaning can be performed and a place to hang wet clothes and boots to dry.

Sometimes there is no drinkable water available but water bottles can be purchased. As everything is usually carried by helicopter to the hut, prices tend to be really high, specially in Switzerland.

The use of boots inside the hut is not allowed. Guests are required to take them off and borrow some Crocs or similar. Boots are left at the entrance along with crampons, ice-axes and climbing material. Only the light equipment is carried inside the hut and dormitories.

NOT ONLY THE TOUR

Many hikers go directly from the airport to the starting point of the route and directly back to the airport when finished. Unfortunately, in so doing, they miss most of the beautiful and interesting places along the way to the tour. Although this book is not intended as a tourist guide, some indications are provided here to help do some research as spending one or more extra days in the surrounding area can be a very rewarding experience.

More detailed information can be found on the internet or at the tourism offices.

For example the evening after the tour, instead of proceeding directly to the airport, the hikers can descend to Martigny, visit the city nd enjoy a Swiss fondue and the following day in the morning, a bike can be borrowed to spend the morning cycling, then swim in a lake, prepare a barbecue, return the bike at Sion, visit the castle and from there take the train in the afternoon to the airport.

INTERESTING PLACES:

–   Martigny (Switzerland): this small city is the last big place along the route when arriving from Switzerland and is well worth a half day visit. Some hotels can be found to spend the night just before or after the tour.

- Fondation Giannada. One of the finest art museums and probably the best ancient car collection in Switzerland
- Museum of the Saint Bernard dogs
- Roman amphitheatre and ruins
- Sion (Switzerland):
  - Domaine des Îles: a lake with green grass, beach volley fields and barbecue spots
  - Tourbillon Castle
- Aosta (Italy):
  - Architecture from Roman times
- Vevey (Switzerland): a very nice city by lake Geneva (Lac Leman for French speakers) with views over the mountains. The global headquarters of Nestlé is located in this town.
  - Nest museum
  - Chaplin museum
- Montreux (Switzerland): another lovely town on the shores of lake Geneva
  - Statue of Freddie Mercury and Queen museum inside the casino
  - Château Chillon
  - Walking path near the lake
- Geneva (Switzerland):
  - United Nations
  - Water jet
  - English garden
  - Cathedral
  - CERN

- Lausanne (Switzerland):
  - The cathedral
  - Olympic museum
- Milan (Italy):
  - Duomo cathedral
  - Gallery Vittorio Emanuele II
  - Teatro alla Scala
  - Sforzesco Castle
- Turin (Italy):
  - Royal Palace
  - Egyptian museum
- Other cities in north Italy:
  - Parma
  - Cremona
  - Modena

OTHER IDEAS:

- Try Swiss chocolate, fondue or raclette.
- Discover some of the famous Swiss cheeses or the wine from Valais.
- Enjoy the delicious Italian gastronomy: pasta, cheese, meat, vegetables...
- Swim in lake Leman with views over the mountains.
- Instead of the direct train/road in Switzerland, make a detour or part of the way by ship in lake Geneva.
- Purchase some food at the supermarket for a barbecue on the shore of the lake.

- North of Italy is one of the most interesting areas in the world for art and architecture. In those cities there are almost always cultural spectacles such as opera, ballet or theater. Milan and Turin also have excelent soccer teams.
- Valaisroule or Wallisrollt. This iniatitive offers bikes to rent or even borrow for free. They can be returned at the same or at a different station along the Rhône river (only in Valais area). The terrain is almost completely plain and there are plenty of cycling paths, many of them separated from cars. Reservation in advance may be needed and closing time is quite early.
- Montreux jazz festival.
- In summer in Switzerland there are a lot of music festivals with famous groups participating, even at small cities such as Sierre or Sion.
- Some ski resorts not far from the route (Verbier, Crans Montana, Champèry...) offer a lot of fun summer activities such as mountain bike, paragliding, going up using the lifts and descend on scooter or some other vehicles...
- Vias ferratas: In Mauvoisin there are two not difficult via ferratas. Gear can be rented at the Hotel-restaurant. Some other via ferratas can be found not far away from the route, in Sion, Champéry or Leysin, for example. Gear can be usually rented at shops nearby.

MORE HIKING:

-   Cabane Chanrion is on Tour of Great Dams (Tour des Grands Barrages), described in other guide in this series of books. These two tours can be easily combined to form a two weeks trek. Other eight or nine day alternatives are also possible.

-   Via Francigena. This trail follows an ancient route that goes from England to Rome. A part of this route is shared with Tour of Combins between Bourg Saint Bernard and Saint Rhèmy. Col du Grand Saint Bernard is the main mountain pass in Via Francigena as it is not a mountain hike but a pilgrim route much like Camino de Santiago. This route may be followed either through north Italy towards Rome or through Switzerland, following Lac Geneva towards London.

-   Cabane de Mille and Mauvoisin are on the Haute Route from Chamonix to Zermatt. These routes can be combined or some of the stages on Haute Route can be added to Tour of Combins to compose a longer route

-   There are many other hiking routes a few kilometres away from this route. Some of them are described on other guides in this series of books.

USEFUL INFORMATION

CURRENCY

In Switzerland the currency is CHF (Swiss francs) and in Italy the currency is Euro.

Euro is sometimes accepted at Swiss restaurants, huts, shops... but at a very unfair change.

Money can be changed at train stations or obtained from cash machines. Cards are generally not accepted in huts or buses, so it is better to get enough cash in Swiss francs and euros before starting the tour.

Some extra expenses could be neccesary and banks, cash machines and exchange facilities are not available during the tour. Aosta and Martigny are the last points where they can be found.

VISA

Hiking this tour involves being and spending some nights in Italy and Switzerland. Italy is member of the European Union and Switzerland is in Schengen area. The tour crosses the border betweeen these countries twice. Passport controls are seldom performed at col du Grand Saint Bernard and Fenêtre du Durand, nevertheless, hikers coming from other countries need to have legal permit for both countries.

WEATHER

In the Alps, the weather is often rainy in summer. Blue skies for six days in a row seldom happen. Most probably, some cloudy and rainy days will happen, and perhaps peaks will not be visible. Unfortunately this is always a risk when hiking in mountains.

Waterproof clothes and a waterproof cover for the backpack are indispensable. They must be able to keep the backpack and the hiker dry for several hours under the rain. Nevertheless, even the best boots get wet after enough time.

Weather is more difficult to predict in mountains than in cities and most online websites in general do not offer accurate forecasts, specially for several days ahead. A useful link is provided later in this guide and also, the weather forecast is usually displayed at the huts on a blackboard or can be directly asked to the staff.

LANGUAGES

Italian and French are the native languages in this area.
Hut keepers, bus drivers and personnel working on the railways generally have a good command of English language.

ORIENTATION, MAPS, GPS

Both in Italy and in Switzerland yellow arrows and yellow rhombus are often painted on rocks and trees to indicate the way. Along this route, often the rhombus have black borders and contain the text "TDC" (Tour des Combins).

In Switzerland the mark for a hiking route consists of a red line between two white lines and for a mountain hiking route consists of a blue line between two white lines. In the international system, a white line and a red line indicate GR (Grand Route).
Hiking paths in Switzerland are indicated by means of metal yellow signals. Almost at every crossing, directions are provided and often an estimated walking time is also indicated (pauses not included). Sometimes marks are yellow metal rhombus with a black walker inside.

 In general, the signalization along this tour is very good. Nevertheless, a paper map and a compass are always advisable when hiking in mountains. The usual scale for hiking maps is 1:50.000.
A very nice map is produced by the Swiss Federal Office for Topography   (Grand St. Bernard-Combins-Arolla, map number 5027T).
This Office publishes excellent online maps including very useful tools, such as draw and measure on maps, export GPS traks...but internet connection is required.

An altimeter is an advisable complement to a compass and a map. Barometric altimeters must be calibrated at huts or at given references to compensate weather conditions.

GPS systems and mobile apps are easier and faster to use than maps and compass, but should not repalce them. Cold temperatures can affect the batteries and often recharging is not possible.
Note: Some mobile apps require mobile coverage to work. In other words, maps are only available when online. If any of these systems is going to be used it is advisable to check them in advance with no connection.

GPS tracks of the route can be found on the internet or can be prepared by the user with the help of a computer (see websites for maps in useful links section). Regardless the source, they should also be checked beforehand.

In some sections the path is not evident and can be marked only by small groups of stones. In those areas it is advisable to walk a small distance, stop, look for the next group of stones and then continue walking. That way of progressing helps avoid correcting the way each few metres or missing some signal.

Note: Tracking and GPS apps consume a lot of energy. Mobile batteries usually are empty after only a few hours hiking. Extra batteries or having several phones in the group is advisable.

TELEPHONE

Mobile coverage is not available in many alpine areas. Sometimes walking some distance to a higher place solves this problem or at least is enough to send an SMS.

International dialing codes: Switzerland 0041, Italy 0039.

Note: at the moment this text was written, Switzerland was not part of the EU roaming agreements, so very high telephone or internet costs may happen.

MILITARY TRAINING ZONES

The Swiss army performs training exercises every summer in mountain areas. In some zones, ammunition can be found by the hikers. Never touch any of these projectiles as some of them can be active and explode.

WATER

Staying hydrated is essential when hiking, specially on sunny days with high temperatures. It is advisable to drink small sips of water periodically. Fortunately, drinkable water of a very high quality is often available during this tour. There are plenty of small streams in the mountains where fresh water can be found.

Places where water is stopped, such as small ponds, must be avoided. Also, when cows can be found around or upstream, water can be polluted by pathogens from manure. The same happens in areas not far away from farms and zones from where flocks can be seen in higher places along the valley.

Water that is obtained directly or almost directly from glaciers is often considered not drinkable as it does not contain enough minerals. Nevertheless some authors say it is compensated by salts present in food.

At Cabane Chanrion water is considered not drinkable and the area betweeen this hut and Mauvoisin is often used to grow cattle. In addition, not far from Cabane Champillon, cows are herded, but drinkable water is available at this hut.

A water bottle is a basic piece of equipment. One litre per person is the absolute minimum and it is advisable to refill as often as possible in order to keep always some reserve. Some persons are used to drink more water than others, so some hikers prefer to have a second bottle despite the extra weight.
Portable water treatment devices and pills can be carried, but in general they are rarely used by hikers in this route.

USEFUL LINKS

ACCOMODATION

-   Cabane de Mille:
    www.cabanedemille.ch
    +41 (0) 27 783 11 82
    info@cabanedemille.ch

-   Cabane Marcel Brunet (no night is spent
    here on the standard route):
    www.cabanebrunet.ch
    +41 (0) 27 778 18 10
    info@cabanebrunet.ch

-   Cabane FXB Panossière:
    www.panossiere.ch
    +41 (0) 27 771 33 22
    info@panossiere.ch

-   Hotel de Mauvoisin (no night is spent here
    on the standard route):
    www.hoteldemauvoisin.ch
    +41 (0) 27 778 11 30
    info@hoteldemauvoisin.ch

-   Cabane Chanrion:
    www.chanrion.ch
    +41 (0) 27 778 12 09
    info@chanrion.ch

- Cabane Champillon (Adolphe Letey):
  www.rifugio-champillon.it
  +39 320 2253 348
  rifugiochampillon@gmail.com

- Saint Rhèmy:
  - o Hotel des Alpes (St Rhèmy Bosses)
    www.desalpeshotel.com
    +39 016 5780 818
    info@desalpeshotel.com

  - o Hotel Suisse (Saint Rhèmy)
    www.suissehotel.it
    +39 016 5780 901
    info@suissehotel.it

- Col du Grand Saint Bernard (no night is
  spent here on the standard route):
  - o Auberge de l'Hospice:
    www.aubergehospice.ch
    +41 (0) 27 787 11 53

- Bourg Saint Pierre (no night is spent here
  on the standard route):
  - o Auberge les Charmettes:
    www.les-charmettes.ch
    +41 (0) 27 787 11 50
    info@les-charmettes.ch

  - o Bivouac Napoleon:
    www.bivouac.ch
    +41 (0) 27 787 11 62
    info@bivouac.ch

MAPS
  – Federal Office of Topography (maps shop):
    http://shop.swisstopo.admin.ch/en/

  – Federal Office of Topography (access to
    online maps):
    www.swisstopo.admin.ch

WEATHER
  – Federal Office of Meteorology and
    Climatology MeteoSwiss (weather
    forecast):
    www.meteoswiss.admin.ch

TRANSPORT
  – SBB/CFF (public transport in Switzerland):
    www.sbb.ch

  – Rome2Rio (transports worlwide):
    www.rome2rio.com

  – Alpentaxi (taxi service):
    www.alpentaxi.ch

  – Societá Valdostana Autoservizi Pubblici
    (bus service in Aosta Valley):
    www.svap.it

  – Skyscanner (search flights, cars rentals, and
    hotels):
    www.skyscanner.net

GPS TRACKS
– Camptocamp:
www.camptocamp.org

– Wikiloc:
www.wikiloc.com

MOBILE MAPPING APPS
– Swiss Map Mobile

– Oruxmaps

OTHER MOBILE APPS
– Peakfinder. This app is useful to identify
the mountains in the background.

– REGA. Helicopter rescue.

EMERGENCIES
– Italy: European Emergency Number 112
– Switzerland: REGA helicopter rescue: 1414
Emergencies: 144

SAFETY IN MOUNTAINS

Hiking is much less dangerous than alpinism, climbing, ski touring or other mountain sports. Nevertheless accidents are always possible. Loose stones, snow and slippery grass or rocks can often be found. Risks are much higher when hiking out of marked tracks or when the weather is rainy or foggy. Glaciers are specially dangerous due to seracs and crevasses. Never venture into glaciers without proper experience and equipment.

A mobile telephone with enough battery to call emergency number (112 in Italy, 144 in Switzerland and 1414 for Rega helicopter rescue) must always be at hand.
Rescue services will ask for information as accurate as possible about:
- what happened
- how many persons are involved in the accident
- how many persons are in the group
- type of accident, severity, conditions of injured people
- what happened
- when
- where
- weather conditions
- possible dangers for helicopter (electric cables for instance)

After calling, stay available near the phone as the emergency services may try to contact back.

For emergencies, the international distress signal consists of six blasts on a whistle or six flashes of light in the night evenly separated for around one minute followed by one minute of silence. It must be repeated until a response is obtained (three blasts per minute followed by one minute of silence).

Heatstrokes and sunburnts can happen if not adequately protected. It is essential to drink water abundantly, use sun cream, and wear sunglasses and hats, specially, but not only on sunny days.

Note: an insurance is highly advisable as being rescued in mountains can be very expensive. Check in advance that Switzerland is covered and what to do, which number to call in case of an accident.

PART II

THE ROUTE

MAP

CLOCKWISE OR COUNTERCLOCKWISE?

It is perfectly possible to hike this tour clockwise or counterclockwise although most of the hikers choose clockwise direction. Views are amazing in both direction.

In short, in counterclockwise direction the tour is a bit harder. Also the first day is quite hard for a starting day, while the last day may be too short.

On the other hand, a short last stage may be more interesting if the hikers plan to fly that same day or to have more time available in the evening for some tourism or other activities.

To lengthen the first day in clockwise direction (or the last in counterclockwise), it is possible to climb Mount Rogneux from Cabane de Mille, what would add about three hours to the stage.

In the next two pages summary charts indicating distances and estimated times for each stage and graphics indicating times between places where accomodation is available are shown.

Some hikers could modify some of the stages and spend a night at Cabane Brunet or Col du Grand Saint Bernard.

CLOCKWISE TOUR					
	START	FINISH	DIST,	CLIMB	TIME
1	Bourg St. Pierre	Cabane de Mille	10,5 km	1.160 m	4h 20 m
2	Cabane de Mille	Cab. Panossière	13,5 km	840 m	5h 10 m
3a	Cab. Panossière	Cabane Chanrion	15,5 km	1.160 m	7h 20 m
3b	Cab. Panossière	Cabane Chanrion	17,1 km	1.338 m	7h 30 m
4	Cabane Chanrion	Cab. Champillon	23 km	1.165 m	7h 50 m
5	Cab. Champillon	St. Rhèmy	15,5 km	630 m	5h 25 m
6	St. Rhèmy	Bourg St. Pierre	18,2 km	1.010 m	5h 40 m

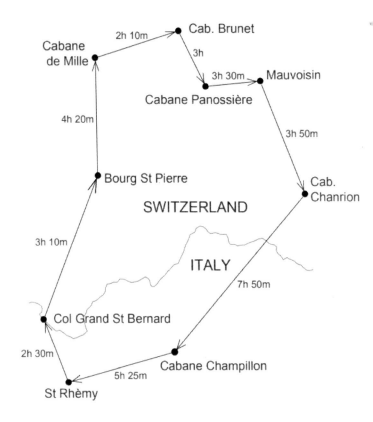

COUNTERCLOCKWISE TOUR					
	START	FINISH	DIST,	CLIMB	TIME
1	Bourg St. Pierre	St. Rhèmy	18,2 km	1.007 m	6h
2	St. Rhèmy	Cab. Champillon	15,5 km	1.476 m	6h 35m
3	Cab. Champillon	Cabane Chanrion	23 km	1.162 m	7h 55 m
4a	Cabane Chanrion	Cab. Panossière	15,5 km	1.343 m	7h 25 m
4b	Cabane Chanrion	Cab. Panossière	17,1 km	1.521 m	7h 40 m
5	Cab. Panossière	Cabane de Mille	13,5 km	668 m	4h 50 m
6	Cabane de Mille	Bourg St. Pierre	10,5 km	317 m	3h 25 m

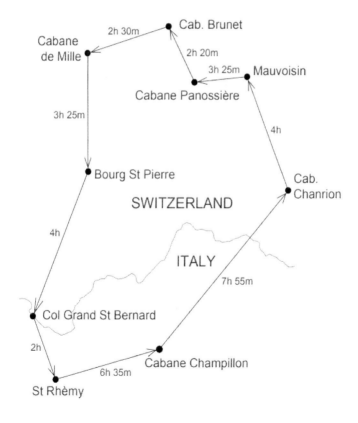

NOTES

In the next two sections, for each stage, a fast fact chart, a description and an elevation profile are provided.
Heights have been obtained from topographic maps and times are approximations for effective walking time for a fit adult. Getting prepared, pauses, breaks for picnic, stops to make photos, time spent checking GPS or maps and others are not included.

For the longest stages, the actual progress is often slower at the end of the day. Rain, mud or poor visibility tend to decrease the rythm too. Some hikers tend to accumulate fatigue and walk more slowly during the last days while others seem to get fitter and advance faster.
For these reasons, every trip and every group is different, so times indicated in this guide can only be orientative. It is advisable to check the rythm of the group in the first stages to improve the forecast for the next stages.

Directions right or left in the descriptions refer to the direction of travel.

THE TOUR CLOCKWISE

This is the standard direction with start and finish at Bourg Saint Pierre.

STAGE 1: BOURG SAINT PIERRE – CABANE DE MILLE

Distance: 10,5 km
Time: 4 hours 20 minutes
Elevation Gain: 1.160 m
Elevation Loss: 317 m
Start Point: Bourg Saint Pierre (1.630 m)
Finish Point: Cabane de Mille (2.473 m)

This stage is the easiest in this tour and provides a good start to adapt before facing more difficult ones. Although quite short in time and never very steep, it involves climbing over one thousand metres.

The route starts at Bourg Saint Pierre (1.630 m), the last village in the valley (Val d'Entremont) before the road climbs to Col du Grand St Bernard, the pass between Italy and Switzerland.
The bus stop is located in front of the hotel-restaurant Auberge les Charmettes. There, some yellow signals indicate the direction of the tour. The path follows the right side of the valley heading north, climbing from 1.632 to reach 2.227 metres at Boveire d'en Bas.

From Boveire d'en Bas, the course continues to Le Coeur (2.238 m) at more or less the same altitude and then climbs to La Vuardette (2.450 m). From there it descends about 200 metres and then goes up to Col de Mille (2.471 m) always following the right side of the valley. Cabane de Mille is a few metres away from Col de Mille.

If the hikers find this stage a bit short, it is possible to leave the backpack at the hut and ascend to Mont Rogneux (3.031 m). This is a blue and white marked mountain path and climbing and returning to the hut takes about three hours.

Cabane de Mille is a comfortable hut that was modernised and renovated in 2.015. It has a very nice dining room and showers are available.

	ALTITUDE (m)	TIME (min)
Bourg Saint Pierre	1.630	0
Chapelle N.D. Lorette	1.630	15
Creux du Má	1.975	90
Boveire d'en Bas	2.227	140
Le Coeur	2.238	165
La Vuardette	2.450	210
Cabane de Mille	2.473	260

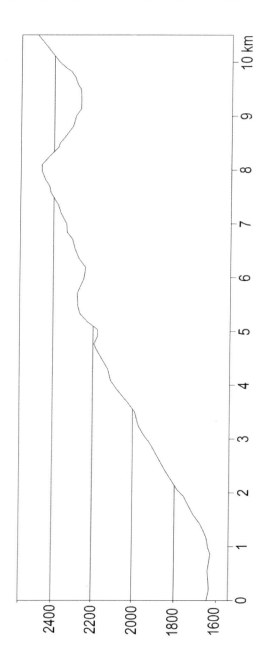

STAGE 2: CABANE DE MILLE – CABANE FXB PANOSSIÈRE

Distance: 13,5 km
Time: 5 hours 10 minutes
Elevation Gain: 840 m
Elevation Loss: 668 m
Start Point: Cabane de Mille (2.473 m)
Finish Point: Cabane FXB Panossière (2.645 m)

The second stage of the tour is one of the easiest too; longer than the first one, but with a smaller elevation gain. The first part of the stage consists of an easy descent followed by a quite horizontal part, in a terrain similar to the previous day. The last part of the stage is more difficult, when the route enters the valley formed by the glacier de Corbassière and in high mountain terrain.

From Cabane de Mille (2.473 m) the path forms a big clockwise curve up to Cabane Brunet. First it descends around four hundred metres and then continues more or less at a constant elevation.
Cabane Brunet is a good point to make a stop for picnic. Some drinks or pie can be bought there.

After Cabane Brunet (2.103 m), the path turns to the right and goes on approximately at the same altitude, crosses a river (Dyure de Sery, 2.150 m) and turns left, going around Becca de Sery clockwise and climbing to 2.344 m.

The path then crosses Glacier de Corbassière over a suspended bridge (height 70 m, lenght 190 m) and then follows climbing up parallel to the glacier to arrive to Cabane FXB Pannosière (2.645 m).
From this hut and its terrace there are probably the most impressing views over the glacier and the Massif des Combins to be found during this tour. Showers are available at an extra cost.

- Alternative: From Cabane Brunet take the path to Col des Avouillons (2.648 m) going around Becca de Sery counterclockwise. This detour adds about forty five minutes to the standard route.

- Note: once at Panossière, backpacks can be left at the hut to climb to Col des Avouillons or the morraine on the right side of the glacier (west side) can be followed up to 3.100 m. This is the route followed by alpinists climbing Tournelon Blanc.

- Note: hiking on glaciers can be mortally dangerous due to crevasses, slippery surfaces and fall of seracs. Venturing on glaciers must be avoided if not experienced and carrying the adequate material (rope, crampons, helmet, ice-axe...)

	ALTITUDE (m)	TIME (min)
Cabane de Mille	2.473	0
Servay	2.074	70
Cabane Brunet	2.103	130
Suspended Bridge	2.360	250
Cabane Panossière	2.645	310

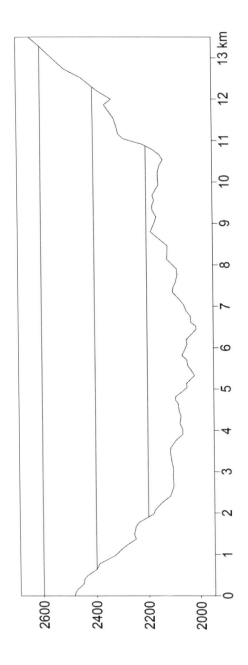

STAGE 3: CABANE FXB PANOSSIÈRE – CABANE CHANRION

Distance: 15,5 km / 17,1 km
Time: 7 h 20 min / 7 h 30 min
Elevation Gain: 1.160 m / 1.338 m
Elevation Loss: 1.343 m / 1.521 m
Start Point: Cabane Panossière (2.645 m)
Finish Point: Cabane Chanrion (2.462 m)

This stage consists of a steep climb to Col des Otannes, a steep descent to Mauvoisin. From there two alternatives are described to Cabane Chanrion.

The route starts following a path that goes parallel to the left side of the glacier and turns to the left to climb steeply to Col des Otannes (2.845 m). This pass is a good spot to watch chamois and marmots (see note below). From Col des Otanes, the course goes down with breathtaking views over the mountains for around one hour and a half and gets to Pazagnou (2.085 m).

At Pazagnou there are two options that require approximately the same time to get to Chanrion.

The first one descends to Mauvoisin, where there is a small and nice restaurant. This point is attainable by bus and road and is good for lunch.
From Mauvoisin, the path climbs, sometimes quite steeply, along tunnels inside the structure of the dam.

Then, it crosses over it and follows the left shore of lake Mauvoisin for about two kilometres. Impressive waterfalls and jets of water can be seen from this area. The path turns to the left and climbs quite steeply to about 2.200 m.

From there it follows up the valley ascending not so steeply to Col de Tsofeiret (2.620 m) and from there descends to Cabane Chanrion (2.462 m).

The second alternative instead of descending to Mauvoisin, climbs to about 2.360 m and follows a path along the valley to Les Roses (2.108 m) where it crosses a river, continues to the ancient Glacier de la Tsessette (2.568 m), descends to the river (Dranse de Bagnes, which crosses at Pont du Lancet 2.040 m) and climbs to Cabane Chanrion (2.462 m).

Note: A third option would be, from the top of the dam a path that goes close to the right shore of the lake parallel to the second alternative and joins it just before climbing to the cabane at 2.042 metres. This would reduce about fifteen minutes the total hike.

- Note: Cabane Chanrion is shared with Haute Route, one of the most popular hiking routes in the Alps which goes from Chamonix to Zermatt. During high season, this hut may be quite crowded.

- Note: the zone between Col des Otanes and about three kilometres before arriving to Chanrion is a faune protected area. Hiking out of the marked tracks is not allowed and dogs must be kept leashed.

- Note: water at Cabane Chanrion is not potable. Some torrents not far from the hut descend at a very high speed, so the water carries a lot of sand and small stones and herds of cows are often present around lake Mauvoisin. It is advisable to refill water previously, for instance near Pazagnou.

- Note: snow can often be found around Col des Otanes, specially early in the season.

- Note: the first and third routes take along tunnels inside the structure of the dam. They are not difficult or dangerous, but progress is slower than along normal paths.

OPTION A		
	ALTITUDE (m)	TIME (min)
Cabane Panossière	2.645	0
Col des Otanes	2.845	40
Pázagnou	2.140	120
Mauvoisin (bus)	1.841	150
Mauvoisin (dam)	1.974	210
Les Fontanes	2.300	310
Cabane Chanrion	2.462	440

OPTION B		
	ALTITUDE (m)	TIME (min)
Cabane Panossière	2.645	0
Col des Otanes	2.845	40
Pázagnou	2.140	120
Les Rosses	2.180	200
La Tsessette	2.568	305
Pont du Lancet	2.040	370
Cabane Chanrion	2.462	450

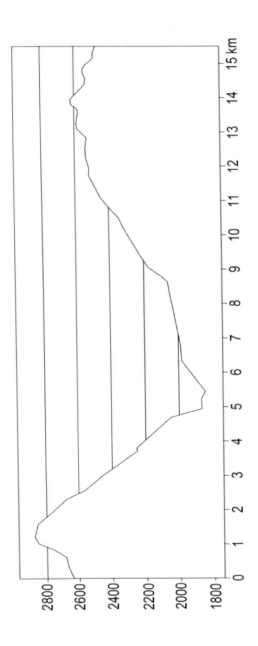

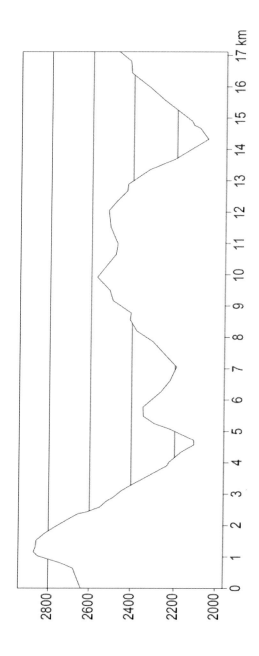

STAGE 4: CABANE CHANRION – CABANE CHAMPILLON

Distance: 23 km
Time: 7 hours 50 minutes
Elevation Gain: 1.165 m
Elevation Loss: 1.162 m
Start Point: Cabane Chanrion (2.462 m)
Finish Point: Cabane Champillon (2.465 m)

This stage is the longest in distance in the tour and comprises two different parts: the climb from Cabane Chanrion to Fenêtre de Durand and then a long descent following the valley in Italy and a short steep ascent to Cabane Champillon.

First part: From the hut, the path descends to the same river that was crossed the previos day (Dranse de Bagnes) but crosses upstream, at 2.181m. From there it goes up to Fenêtre de Durand (2.797 m) along the right side of the ancient glacier valley for about two hours. Almost no vegetation can be found in this area except for some small flowers.
At Fenêtre de Durand the tour enters in Aosta valley. This route was used during the Second World War by people scaping from Italy to Switzerland. Some informative pannels are installed near the pass.

Second part: the path descends the valley describing several curves, arriving to Champillon village (2.080 m) and then ascending steeply to the hut.

There is no difficulty in this part except for the long distance to cover and the fact that signalling can be confusing or not present at some points. During the descent, it is important to check the map or GPS as several paths go down and it is possible to miss the way, specially if visibility is poor.

The Italian side is dryer and less high mountain than the stages on the Swiss side. Water may be more difficult to find although there are several streams along this stage.

- Note: Cheese can be bought from local producers at some of the small huts just before arriving to Cabane Champillon.

- Note: Rockfalls may happen at the southeastern slopes of Mont Gelé, not far from Fenêtre de Durand. Avoid exploring this area out of the marked paths.

- Note: Cabane Champillon offers a very cozy and easy-going environment and dinner and breakfast are specially nice in this hut. Showers are available.

	ALTITUDE (m)	TIME (min)
Cabane Chanrion	2.462	0
Fenètre de Durand	2.797	155
Alpe des Toules	2.378	225
Balme	2.128	270
By	2.009	290
Champillon	2.080	400
Cabane Champillon	2.465	470

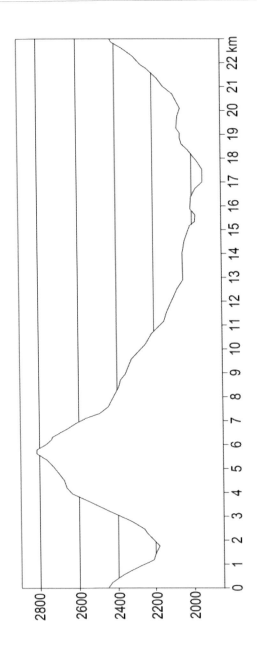

STAGE 5: CABANE CHAMPILLON – SAINT RHÈMY

Distance: 15,5 km
Time: 5 hours 25 minutes
Elevation Gain: 630 m
Elevation Loss: 1.476 m
Start Point: Cabane Champillon (2.465 m)
Finish Point: Saint Rhèmy (1.619 m)

The main difficulty of this stage is the climb to Col Champillon in the beginning of the day. Then, it consists mainly in following the path along the valley, first descending, then following almost at the same altitude and finally descending more steeply to Saint Rhèmy.

From Cabane Champillon (2.465 m) the route ascends to Col Champillon (2.709 m). This is a quite step climb. From the Col there is another steep descent on the other side. At around 2.250 m the path to the right must be taken. It continues gently for around one kilometre and then descends steeply to 1.800 m and crosses a small river (Torrent de Menouvre). From there, the route climbs about one hundred metres and then follows the valley without big ascents or descents for several kilometres mostly surrounded by forest. Then it descends forming some curves and turns to the right to arrive to Saint Rhèmy (1.619 m). Saint Rhèmy is a small village, even smaller than Bourg Saint Pierre.

In Saint Rhèmy some hotels can be found or it is possible to continue to Saint Rhèmy en Bosses (1.644 m) or even to Saint Léonard (1.519 m), but this distance must be regained the following day. These are standard hotels, not mountain huts as at the end of the other stages.

The signalization of this stage can be confusing at some points. The use of a GPS or map is advisable.

Saint Rhèmy can be more convenient as a start/finish point of the tour for travellers who arrive from Italy.

	ALTITUDE (m)	TIME (min)
Cabane Champillon	2.465	0
Col Champillon	2.708	60
Magna Pointier	1.809	160
Magna Barasson	1.865	255
Saint Rhèmy	1.619	325

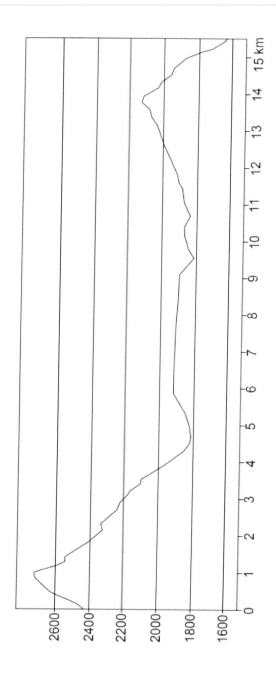

STAGE 6: SAINT RHÈMY – BOURG SAINT PIERRE

Distance: 18,2 km
Time: 5 hours 40 minutes
Elevation Gain: 1.010 m
Elevation Loss: 1.007 m
Start Point: Saint Rhèmy (1.619 m)
Finish Point: Bourg Saint Pierre (1.630 m)

This stage comprises two different parts. First, on the Italian side, a long and not very steep climb from Saint Rhèmy to Col du Grand Saint Bernard and afterwards another long and less steep descent on the Swiss side from the pass to Bourg Saint Pierre.

From Saint Rhèmy the path follows close to the river for about one kilometre. At Thoules (1.721 m) there are two choices: to continue along the path that runs parallel to the river and later climbs more steeply or to cross the road and follow the path that climbs into the forest to around 2.000 m and then turns to the left and follows the valley at an almost constant elevation. Both paths join at about 2.150 m to carry on going up the valley and arrive to Col du Grand Saint Bernard (2.469 m). The main road is crossed three times.

At Col du Grand Saint Bernard there are several interesting points: the statue of Saint Bernard, the hospice, the lake and some souvenirs shops.

At the Auberge, food and drinks can be purchased. This is a good point to make a pause, but probably hikers will arrive early for lunch.

The path down towards Bourg Saint Pierre goes first on the right side of the valley and then crosses the road and continues on the left side passing close to Lac des Toules (1.809 m). The main road is on the opposite side of the valley and the structure for the car tunnel can be seen while hiking.

Note: the area between Torrents des Erbets (about one and a half kilometres after arriving to Lac des Toules) and Bourg Saint Pierre is a faune protected area. Hiking out of the marked tracks is not allowed and dogs must be kept leashed. Marmots and other wild animals are often spotted in this area.

- Note: In 1.800 Napoleon crossed the Alps with his army through Col du Grand Saint Bernard to invade Italy. French artists Jacques-Louis David and Paul Delaroche painted very different portraits of that moment. Some informative panels can be seen near the col and in Bourg Saint Pierre.

	ALTITUDE (m)	TIME (min)
Saint Rhèmy	1.619	0
Col Grand St Bernard	2.469	150
La Pierre	2.039	220
Barrage des Toules	1.730	290
Bourg Saint Pierre	1.632	340

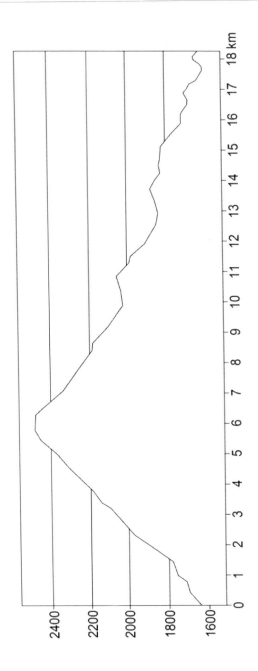

THE TOUR
COUNTERCLOCKWISE

This is the less common direction with start and finish in Bourg Saint Pierre.

STAGE 1: BOURG SAINT PIERRE – SAINT RHÈMY

Distance: 18,2 km
Time: 6 hours
Elevation Gain: 1.007 m
Elevation Loss: 1.010 m
Start Point: Bourg Saint Pierre (1.632 m)
Finish Point: Saint Rhèmy (1.619 m)

This first stage comprises two parts. First, on the Swiss side, a long and not very steep climb from Bourg Saint Pierre to Col du Grand Saint Bernard and afterwards another long and steeper descent on the Italian side from the Col du Grand Saint Bernard to Saint Rhémy.

From Bourg Saint Pierre, the route goes down to the river and crosses it at 1.591 m. Then it turns to the left and climbs along the right side of the valley, passing close to Lac des Toules (1.809 m). The main road is on the opposite side of the valley and the structure of the tunnels for the cars can be seen while hiking.

At La Pierre (2.039 m), the route follows the path to
the right. This path crosses the river (Dranse
d'Entremont) and the road and goes on climbing,
now on the left side of the valley to arrive to Col du
Grand Saint Bernard (2.469 m).

At Col du Grand Saint Bernard there are several
interesting points:
- The statue of Saint Bernard
- The hospice
- The lake

From the Col, going down on the Italian side, the
path crosses the road three times. Around five
hundred metres after the third time, at about 2.150
m, there are two possible options:
a) The path to the left continues descending for
about two kilometres, enters the forest and then
descends steeply to Saint Rhèmy.
b) The path to the right descends more steeply,
arrives at Thoules (1.721 m) and then follows the
valley, not far from the river to the small village of
St Rhèmy.

At Saint Rhèmy (1.619 m) some hotels can be found
or it is possible to continue to Saint Rhèmy en
Bosses (1.644 m), or even Saint Léonard (1.519 m),
but this distance must be regained the following
day. These are standard hotels, not a mountain huts
as at the end of the other stages.

-Note: the area between Bourg Saint Pierre and Torrents des Erbets (about one kilometre after arriving to Lac des Toules) is a faune protected area. Hiking out of the marked tracks is not allowed and dogs must be kept leashed. Marmots and other wild animals are often spotted in this area.

-Note: Napoleon crossed the Alps with his army in 1.800 through Col du Grand Saint Bernard to invade Italy. French artists Jacques-Louis David and Paul Delaroche painted very different portraits of that moment. Information panels can be found at the col and in Bourg Saint Pierre.

	ALTITUDE (m)	TIME (min)
Bourg Saint Pierre	1.632	0
Barrage des Toules	1.730	60
La Pierre	2.039	150
Col Grand St Bernard	2.469	240
Saint Rhèmy	1.619	360

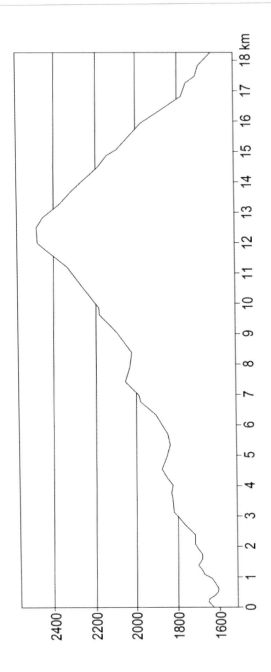

STAGE 2: SAINT RHÈMY – CABANE CHAMPILLON

Distance: 15,5 km
Time: 6 hours 35 minutes
Elevation Gain: 1.476 m
Elevation Loss: 630 m
Start Point: Saint Rhèmy (1.619 m)
Finish Point: Cabane Champillon (2.465 m)

This is quite a long and hard stage due to the elevation gain (almost 1.500 metres). The main difficulties are a quite steep climb in the beginning of the stage near Saint Rhèmy and a another steep climb not far from the end of the day to Col Champillon.

From Saint Rhémy (1.619 m) the path climbs steeply around five hundred metres in a forested area. From there it turns to the right, first descends gently and later continues at almost the same altitude for about eight kilometres following the curves of the valley. In this section the path is wide and without difficulty.

The path crosses a small river (Torrent de Menouvre) at 1.800 m, and after crossing, climbs to Col de Champillon (2.709 m) quite steeply.
Once in the pass, the main difficulties have been overcome. The rest of the stage is a steep descent to Cabane Champillon (2.465 m).

The signalization of this stage, specially during the ascent to Col Champillon is not very clear at some points. The use of a GPS or map is recommended specially in days with poor visibility conditions.

- Note: Cheese can be bought from local producers at some of the small huts near Cabane Champillon.

- Note: Cabane Champillon offers a very cozy, comfortable and easy-going environment and dinner and breakfast are specially nice in this hut. Showers are available.

	ALTITUDE (m)	TIME (min)
Saint Rhèmy	1.619	0
Magna Barasson	1.865	80
Magna Pointier	1.809	170
Col Champillon	2.708	350
Cabane Champillon	2.465	395

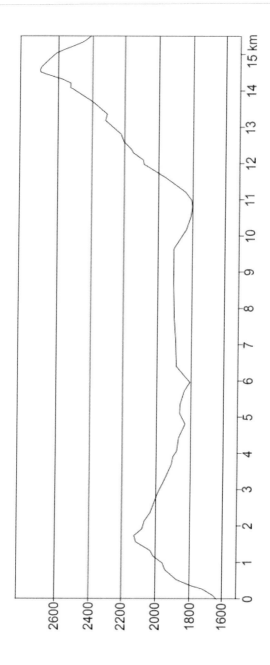

STAGE 3: CABANE CHAMPILLON – CABANE CHANRION

Distance: 23 km
Time: 7 hours 55 minutes
Elevation Gain: 1.162 m
Elevation Loss: 1.165 m
Start Point: Cabane Champillon (2.465 m)
Finish Point: Cabane Chanrion (2.462 m)

This stage is the longest in distance in the tour and comprises two different parts: the climb from Cabane Champillon to Fenêtre de Durand and the descent to Cabane Chanrion.

First part: From the hut, there is a quite steep descent to around 2.000 metres and then the course turns to the left and follows up the side of the valley, first on an easy continuous ascent and later more steeply to Fenêtre de Durand (2.797 m). At the col (2.797 m) the tour enters in Switzerland.
During the ascent, it is important to check the map or GPS as there are several paths in the valley and it is possible to miss the way, specially with foggy weather, as there are several paths and the signalling of this area could be better.

Second part: from the col, the path descends following the left side of the ancient glacier valley and crosses a small river (Dranse de Bagnes, 2.181 m). Then climbs to Cabane Chanrion (2.462 m), where the stage finishes.

Almost no vegetation other than small flowers is found after Fenêtre de Durand.

-Note:Water at cabane Chanrion is not drinkable. It is advisable to fill the bottles in advance.

-Note: This route was used during the Second World War to scape from Italy. Some interesting information panels are installed near the col.

-Note: Rockfalls can happen at the southeastern slopes of Mont Gelé. Exploring in this area out of the marked paths can be dangerous.

	ALTITUDE (m)	TIME (min)
Cabane Champillon	2.465	0
Champillon	2.080	45
By	2.009	145
Balme	2.128	175
Alpe des Toules	2.378	235
Fenêtre de Durand	2.797	340
Cabane Chanrion	2.462	475

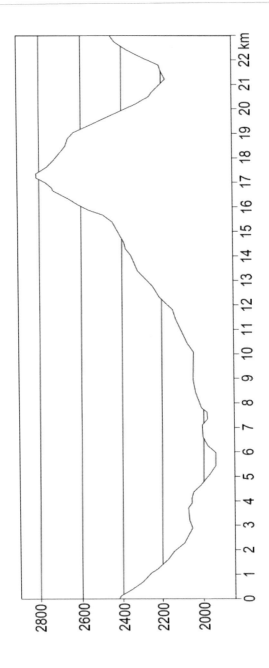

STAGE 4: CABANE CHANRION – CABANE FXB PANOSSIÈRE

Distance: 15,5 km / 17,1 km
Time: 7 hours 25 minutes / 7 hours 40 minutes
Elevation Gain: 1.343 m / 1.521 m
Elevation Loss: 1.160 m / 1.338 m
Start Point: Cabane Chanrion (2.462 m)
Finish Point: Cabane FXB Panossiére (2.645 m)

This stage offers two possibilities. The first is an small an easy climb to col Tsofeiret, a long descent following the right side of the valley to Mauvoisin, a long ascent to Pázagnou and Col des Otanes and a short steep descent to Cabane FXB Panossière. The second one follows the left side of the valley and joins the first alternative at Pázagnou.

First option: From the hut, the path climbs easily to col de Tsofeiret (2.620 m). From there, it descends following the right side of the valley, first gently to 2.200 m and then more steeply to around 2.060 and then it turns to the left to follow closer and parallel to the shore of Lake Mauvoisin for about two kilometres up to the dam. Impressive waterfalls and jets of water can be spotted from this area. The course passes over the dam and then enters into the tunnels of the structure to descend to Mauvoisin (1.841 m). This point is attainable by bus and road and there is a nice restaurant that can be a good place for picnic around noon.From Mauvoisin the route climbs steeply to Pázagnou.

Second option: From Chanrion, the path descends to Pont du Lancet (2.040 m), crosses the river (Dranse de Bagnes), and continues along the left side of the valley, first ascending to La Tsessette (2.568 m), and then descending to Les Roses (2.108 m) from where it climbs again to about 2.360 and descends to Pázagnou (2.140 m).

From Pazagnou the path continues to Col des Otanes (2.845 m).This is a long and steep climb, probably the most difficult of this tour.
Col des Otanes is a good spot to watch chamois and marmots (see note below).
Once at the pass, the rest of the day is easy. The path descends quite steep until close to the glacier, where it turns to the right and follows almost straight to Cabane Panossière. This zone offers probably the best views over Glacier de Corbassière and Massif des Combins. Cabane Panossière has an astounding terrace and showers are available.

- Note: the area between three kilometres after Cabane Chanrion and Col des Otanes is a faune protected area. Hiking out of the marked tracks is not allowed and dogs must be kept leashed.

- Note: hiking on glaciers is an exciting activity but can be mortally dangerous due to crevasses, slippery surfaces and fall of seracs. Avoid venturing in glaciers if not experienced and carrying the adequate material (rope, crampons, helmet, ice-axe...).

- Note: snow can be found near Col des Otanes, specially if early in the season.

- Note: the first and third routes take along tunnels inside the structure of the dam. They are not difficult or dangerous, but progress is slower than along normal paths.

- Note: a third, shorter option, is, from Pont du Lancet, a path that follows the left side of lake Mauvoisin and arrives to the dam and joins the first alternative. This option reduces about fifteen minutes.

OPTION A		
	ALTITUDE (m)	TIME (min)
Cabane Chanrion	2.462	0
Les Fontanes	2.300	110
Mauvoisin (dam)	1.974	190
Mauvoisin (bus)	1.841	240
Pázagnou	2.140	290
Col des Otanes	2.845	415
Cabane Panossière	2.645	445

OPTION B		
	ALTITUDE (m)	TIME (min)
Cabane Chanrion	2.462	0
Pont du Lancet	2.040	55
La Tsessette	2.568	155
Les Rosses	2.108	240
Pázagnou	2.140	305
Col des Otanes	2.845	430
Cabane Panossière	2.645	460

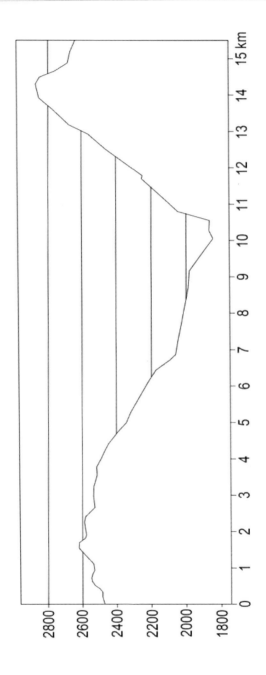

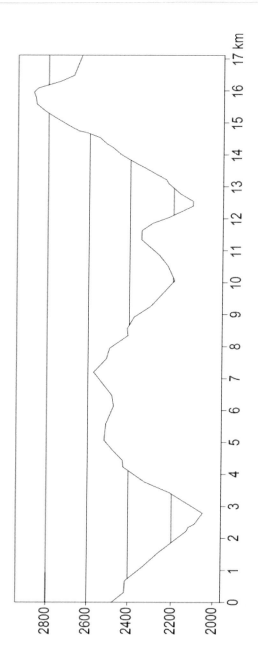

STAGE 5: CABANE FXB PANOSSIÈRE – CABANE DE MILLE

Distance: 13,5 km
Time: 4 hours 50 minutes
Elevation Gain: 668 m
Elevation Loss: 840 m
Start Point: Cabane FXB Panossière (2.645 m)
Finish Point: Cabane de Mille (2.473 m)

Once at Cabane Panossière, the main difficulties of the tour have already been overcome. The first part of this quite easy stage consists in descending the glacier valley, while the second one takes place in a much easier terrain, where the path goes almost at a constant altitude first and then climbs to Cabane de Mille.

From Cabane FXB Panossière (2.645 m), the path descends the valley parallel to Glacier de Corbassière and crosses the glacier river over an imposing suspended bridge (altitude 2.360 m, height 70 m, lenght 190 m).
After the crossing, the route continues to the north descending to around 2.150 m and from there goes down more slowly and crosses a small river (Dyure de Sery at 2.165 m). From that point it goes on approximately at the same altitude to Cabane Brunet (2.103 m).
Cabane Brunet is a good point to make a stop for picnic.

After the hut, the path advances towards the west and then north-west following up the valley on an constant and not very steep climb to Col de Mille (2.473 m). Cabane de Mille is a few meters away from the pass.

A more demanding alternative is available if this stage is considered too easy. After crossing the suspended bridge, there is path that goes through Col des Avouillons (2.648 m) and then from Écuries de Sery (2.232 m) adn continues to Cabane Brunet (this detour adds around thirty minutes) or climbs to Mont Rogneux (3.083 m) and descends to Cabane de Mille via Goli du Rogneux or via Goli d'Aget (this option would add approximately two hours). The last variant includes a difficult mountain path marked blue and white.

	ALTITUDE (m)	TIME (min)
Cabane Panossière	2.645	0
Suspended Bridge	2.360	30
Cabane Brunet	2.103	140
Servay	2.074	200
Cabane de Mille	2.473	290

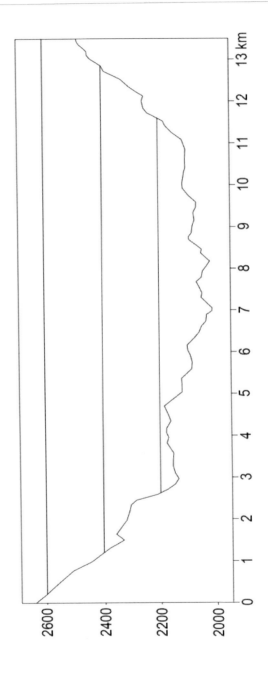

STAGE 6: CABANE DE MILLE – BOURG SAINT PIERRE

Distance: 10,5 km
Time: 3 hours 25 minutes
Elevation Gain: 317 m
Elevation Loss: 1.160 m
Start Point: Cabane de Mille (2.473 m)
Finish Point: Bourg Saint Pierre (1.630 m)

This is by far the easiest stage in the tour. It is a quite long descent from Cabane de Mille to Bourg Saint Pierre following the left side of the valley in south direction.

From the Cabane de Mille (2.473 m) the path descends about 200 metres and then climbs back to La Vuardette (2.450 m). From there it descends to Le Coeur (2.238 m) and continues to Boveire d'en Bas (2.227 m) almost at the same altitude. From that point it continues going down to Creux du Má (1.975 m) and Chapelle Nôtre Dame de Lorette (1.630 m) and finally at almost the same elevation continues about one kilometre to Bourg Saint Pierre.

The stage and the route end at Bourg Saint Pierre, near the bus stop and the hotel-restaurant Auberge des Charmettes where it started.
At Bourg Saint Pierre there are some nice restaurants with terraces where it is possible to enjoy a drink while waiting for the bus.

- Note: for some extra hiking, it is possible to leave the backpack at Cabane de Mille, climb to Mont Rogneux (3.031 m) and return before going down to Bourg Saint Pierre. This mountain path is blue and white marked and adds about three hours to the stage.

	ALTITUDE (m)	TIME (min)
Cabane de Mille	2.473	0
La Vuardette	2.450	50
Le Coeur	2.238	85
Boveire d'en Bas	2.227	110
Creux du Má	1.975	150
Chap. N.D. Lorette	1.630	190
Bourg Saint Pierre	1.630	205

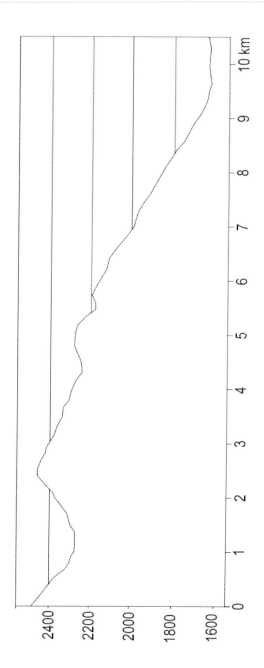

Manufactured by Amazon.ca
Acheson, AB

12870388R00058